The Kite That Braved Old Orchard Beach

Year-Round Poems for Young People

Some Other Books by X. J. Kennedy

BRATS

FRESH BRATS

THE FORGETFUL WISHING WELL:
POEMS FOR YOUNG PEOPLE

THE OWLSTONE CROWN

GHASTLIES, GOOPS & PINCUSHIONS
(Margaret K. McElderry Books)

KNOCK AT A STAR: A CHILD'S INTRODUCTION TO POETRY
(with Dorothy M. Kennedy)

The Kite That Braved Old Orchard Beach

Year-Round Poems for Young People

by X. J. Kennedy
Illustrations by Marian Young

Margaret K. McElderry Books
NEW YORK
Collier Macmillan Canada
TORONTO
Maxwell Macmillan Publishing Group
NEW YORK OXFORD SINGAPORE SYDNEY

For Curly, with love

Margaret K. McElderry Books
Macmillan Publishing Company
866 Third Avenue
New York, NY 10022

Collier Macmillan Canada, Inc.
1200 Eglinton Avenue East
Suite 200
Don Mills, Ontario M3C 3N1
First Edition
Printed in the United States of America
10 9 8 7 6 5 4 3 2 1

Library of Congress Cataloging-in-Publication Data
Kennedy, X. J.
The Kite that braved old Orchard Beach : Year-round poems for
young people / X.J. Kennedy.—1st ed.
p.   cm.
Summary: A collection of poems, grouped in such categories as
"Growing & Dreaming," "Family," "Not So Ordinary Things," and
"Birds, Beasts & Fish."
ISBN 0–689–50507–8
1. Children's poetry, American.   [1. American poetry.]
I. Title.
PS3521.E563K58   1991
90–20100
811'.54—dc20

CONTENTS

THANKS

Several of these poems first appeared in the following anthologies edited by Myra Cohn Livingston: "New Year's Advice from My Cornish Grandmother" in *New Year's Poems* (1987); "Different Dads" in *Poems for Fathers* (1989); "At Plymouth" (formerly called "At the First Thanksgiving") in *Thanksgiving Poems* (1985); "Walking Big Bo" in *Dog Poems* (1990); and "Hot Milk" (formerly called "Grandmother in Winter") in *Poems for Grandmothers* (1990), all published by Holiday House.

"Paperclips" first appeared in *These Small Stones*, edited by Norma Farber and Myra Cohn Livingston (A Charlotte Zolotow Book/Harper & Row, 1987).

"Summer Cooler" first appeared on a bookmark published by the Children's Book Council.

"My Stupid Parakeet Named After You" was suggested by a letter to the author from Robert Crawford.

As always, Dorothy M. Kennedy served as a fine, tough first editor.

Joys

FIRST ONE AWAKE

I like to be the first one up
When everyone's still sleeping,
When in the moonlit morning, night
Is laid by for safekeeping,

When robins stumble out of bed
And yawn wide, when the paper
Slung from the truck bumps our brick porch,
When trails of cloudwhite vapor

Cross from the airport, heading east
To sea, and all the world
Sits waiting like a cocoa cup
That no spoon yet has swirled.

ROLLER COASTERS

From coast to coast some like to fly
Or tack up rock-star posters,
And that's all right, I guess. But I
Like riding roller coasters.

A roller coaster—it's the most.
I love that first huge scare
When you go shooting down to find
You're sitting on thin air.

Old timbers thunder under wheels,
Shrill screams and hollers sound,
While, tilting, round a curve you roar,
A mile from solid ground.

Whiz! up a slightly lower hill!
The cold steel bar shoves hard
Against your two tight-knuckled fists—
Now squeaky brakes bombard

Your ears with squeals—the slowing wheels
Declare your trip all done
And, dizzily, you stagger off—
What misery! What fun!

4

COLLECTING THINGS

In dresser drawers, collector kids
Save old cast-off milk-shake lids,

Slimy birds' nests, strands of string,
This and that and everything:

Peelings from an orange peeled,
Band-Aids from cuts long since healed,

Birthday candles (chewing wax),
Cotton candy, knicks and knacks,

Three-leaf clovers, snakes' shed skin,
Smelly shells some tide dragged in—

What do all those treasures prove?—
"Mom, I need more room! Let's move!"

AIRPORT

People sprinting to and fro
Through this fast-paced palace
On the move to Tel Aviv,
Budapest, or Dallas.

People struggle, lugging bags,
Backpacks, sacks of skis,
Lobsters boxed in swimming pools,
Books from overseas.

Speakers booming hollow booms:
Flight nineteen-oh-nine
Now arriving at gate ten—
Is it yours or mine?

People saying last good-byes
With wet and streaky faces,
People saying warm hellos
With squeeze-'em-tight embraces.

SMALL-TOWN FIREWORKS

No cannon-crackers were ever more loud—
I'll bet they rattled the moons of Mars—
Every baby started bawling.
Ka-bash! went the windshields of six parked cars—
You could hear glass snowflakes falling.

We sucked in our breath. But then an alley
Cat set foot on a delicate wire
And off—to the *oohs* of the crowd—
Went the stars and stripes, all made out of fire,
That should have been saved for the grand finale.

Next a rocket whooshed to the peak of the sky,
But oh! what a spot it picked for its fall:
Right on the roof of the old town hall
Dry as a box of long-kept tinder—
A fireman I know saved me a cinder

And I've packed it away in my special file
Of things to remember a good long while.

POET

Listen, I'm talking in stumbles and bumps—
Let's see if your ears start to tingle.
Over a word's back another word jumps
And when it comes down there's a jingle.

Spaghetti, confetti, and pink lemonade,
Telephones, whales' bones, and weather
Are things that keep tumbling around in my head—
Let's see if they'll all go together.

ROMPING IN THE RAIN

You in your shrunk-tight swimming suit,
   Me in my holey old clothes
      Are getting more wet
      Than we'll ever get
   Under sprinkler or garden hose.

When a cloud's sprung a leak
And it's rained for a week
      And it's planning to rain still more,
         Why, what's left to do
         But go bash right through
      That drizzly old drab downpour?

The first icy pins
Strike our backs and shins—
      It's like making that first cold dive!—
         While, two shrieking banshees
         Or war-whooping Comanches,
      We come on loud and live.

Through a waterfall
A whole sky tall
      We batter and smash and plunge
         Getting sloppier
         And soppier
      Than an ocean-bottom sponge.

We may look a mess
But we've had, I guess,
    More fun than anyone knows—
        You in your shrunk-tight
        Swimming suit,
    Me in my holey old clothes.

Growing
& Dreaming

THE UNICORN I TRIED TO PAINT

The unicorn I tried to paint
Has ended up a cow.
My teacher looked and said, "How quaint."
There's trouble on her brow—

My cow's, I mean. She looks as though
Her horn had slightly slipped.
She has worse problems down below.
My paintbrush must have dripped.

Was such a creature ever born?
I'll keep her anyhow.
She's realer than a unicorn,
My cockeyed unicow.

MY MARSHMALLOWS

Mine are the kind that don't brown—they scorch,
Smoke, smolder, turn to a flaming torch,

The kind a dog happens by to lick,
That don't stay stuck to the sharpest stick

But fall off and grow fur coats of ashes
Or roll in the coals with farewell flashes.

VALUABLES

I found a fossil in a rock:
The print of some lost fern
That died a million years or so
Ago. I had to learn

If it was valuable or not—
I rushed right off to show
Aunt Jessie the geologist—
Could it be rare? *She'd* know.

"A beauty of a specimen,"
She said. (Wow! how intense!
I'd struck it rich!) "It's common, though,
Worth maybe eighty cents."

But now I keep it on my shelf,
Its stone leaves crisp and nice,
With things that matter to me, not
For sale at any price.

MAISIE'S LAMENT

His lips look like cherries,
    His teeth like white pearls,
His eyes are the berries—

    He's some other girl's.

TAKING DOWN THE SPACE-TROLLEY

The whine of our space-trolley along the wire
Strung from our back porch to the maple tree,
Shrill as, at summer's end, a cicada's scream
Won't sound again unless it sounds in dream.

We grew too heavy for it. So at last
Dad took it down and slapped tar on the hole
Left where its hook screwed tight to the tree's bole
And broke off our connection with the past.

THE MAILMAN'S SUCH A MAGIC GUY

The mailman's such a magic guy,
I always run when he's been by—
What star of screen or basketball
Dropped me a letter after all?

Did I get some humongous box
All golden chains and diamond locks
That, creaking wide, will yield at least
Some flame-breathed prehistoric beast?

Of course, the usual kind of mail
Announces some old bargain sale
Or else a card—oh, disappointment!—
Tells me my teeth have an appointment.

GENERATION GAP

The teacher looked at me and frowned
A frown that must have weighed a pound,
And said, "When I was young as you,
There were more things I didn't do."

CIRCUS DREAMS

To memorize
        Old Robert Browning
Is for *some* guys.
        Me, I'll take clowning.

I'll run off, far
        From mathematics
Where I can star
        In acrobatics.

Why, soon crowds will
        Come cheer my handstands!
I bet they'll fill
        A thousand grandstands.

With dancing bears
        I'll rock and roll.
I'll walk high wires
        With cool control,

And while you gape,
        With whip I'll shepherd
From tub through hoop
        Each snarling leopard.

Rolled round and small,
        I'll take quick flights,
A cannonball
        In spangled tights—

20

BOOM! How I'll set
        The whole tent wowing!
Then out of a net
        I'll bounce down, bowing,

And Miss McBride
        Who called me dunce
Will crow with pride,
        "I taught *him* once."

POLAR DREAMS

When I was young—well, younger—
I thought the earth had poles
Like giant posts or redwood trees
That grew like seeds from holes,

That if you went exploring
Far fields of arctic snow
Where frozen winds kept roaring,
You'd bend neck back in awe

At a north pole skyscraper-high,
Real solid wooden stuff
Like clothes poles, barber poles, or poles
To vault with. Sure enough,

In school I looked for those big poles
On a big globe of the world—
Brass posts poked from it, north and south,
So that it might be twirled.

I dreamed that soon, when I got big,
I'd lead an expedition
To climb out on those metal poles.
I'd make it my ambition

To be the first to check them out
And bring back home some rare
New breed of mice, some wet dry-ice,
Or a pink-furred polar bear.

WHAT I USED TO WONDER

A rabbit upright on two legs?
      The strangest of all scenes!
How could he tint a ton of eggs
      And jars of jelly beans?

Now Santa Claus made sense. His home
      Could hold hordes of elf toilers,
But how could rabbit holes have room
      For huge sky-high egg boilers?

I used to puzzle all night long,
      I'd think, "This mystery thickens.
Does he lay all those eggs himself
      Or chum around with chickens?"

Family

DIFFERENT DADS

Training horses, riding fire trucks—
Some dads do that. Other dads
Mostly sit and scribble figures
All day long on paper pads.

Fixing bikes, some fathers falter
Even though for years they've tried.
When they're done, your chain will dangle
Every time you try to ride.

That's why when my bike has problems
I ask Mom. Poor helpless Dad
Can't twist wrenches or ply pliers—
Otherwise, he's not half bad.

Truth is, he's a whiz at adding.
Once when I didn't dig my math
He explained it, writing numbers
In the soapsuds of my bath.

Then there was the time my bedroom
Had a visitor—a bat—
And what superhero trapped it
Gently in my baseball hat?

Father. Could you find one better?
Maybe. But you'd travel far.
Any fathers have their good sides.
Doesn't matter who they are.

27

PACIFIER

Nights when Robert starts to blubber
Mother plugs his mouth with rubber,

A squirmy little chewy knob
He bites on and forgets to sob.

Once I picked one up and bit.
What do babies see in it?

REMEMBERING ICE

"When I was *your* age," Granddad tells me, "ice
Had to be hauled by horse-drawn wagon. Twice
A week it came, in huge blue shiny blocks
Cut to exactly fit in your ice box.
And all us kids, we'd think ourselves in luck
If we could beg one little chunk to suck.
We'd chase the iceman till he'd splinter off
And throw us blizzards of that precious stuff.
With freezing hands, we'd slurp off down the street—
I've never tasted anything so sweet."

I'll bet he knows just how things used to be
When dinosaurs watched black-and-white TV.

TWO-WEEK CAR TRIP

Some traffic jam! It takes a whole
Morning to get to pay our toll.
My heavy metal rock-and-roll
     Tapes don't improve Dad's feelings.
The rest stop's much too mobbed to park.
Once more, with growls, the sky grows dark.
Says Mom, "We'd better build an ark"—
     Can cars get leaky ceilings?

Our bike rack let go of my bike.
It went off pedaling down the pike.
To find it took a two-mile hike
     Through woods and weeds and prickers,
But we could trace which way it went:
It hit a tree and made a dent
And now its handlebars are bent—
     My snerdy sister snickers.

Moondog has made a mess. I scold her.
"That mutt," says Dad, "we should have sold her."
I'm not a good road-map refolder—
     Rip-p-p!—now I've gone and torn it.
We stop for gas and watch a stickup.
Each time we hit a bump I hiccup.
I've got a bite. Where did we pick up
     That mean hitchhiking hornet?

The Methodist Church picnic bus
Keeps honking as it passes us—
Oops! Percival, the little cuss,
    Has squirmed out of his unders.
Mom doesn't beat around the bush:
She flings a towel around his tush
And scowls a scowl that makes us shoosh—
    "You watch him, now!" Dad thunders.

Then suddenly a fearful bang
Is followed by a *clang-clang-clang.*
Dad groans. "We've got a blowout, gang.
    I *knew* these tires were wrecks." It's
A front one. Smell that smoky smell.
What next? Aunt Min lets out a yell—
"We've overshot tonight's motel
    By twenty-seven exits!"

Dad rolls his sleeves up to attack
The tire, the spare tire, and the jack,
But bending, hollers, "Ouch! my back!"
    And falls flat in the gravel.
Whole hours pass. Then we're in luck:
The state police ask, "Are you stuck?"
And send for stretcher and tow truck—
    It's *interesting* to travel!

HOT MILK

When I'd be at play in the smoky-breath cold,
My grandmother'd throw wide her window and scold,
"You come in this minute and get warmed up!
Dry your wet feet. I'll make you a cup

Of nice hot milk." Which might sound kind,
But it wasn't at all what I'd have in mind—
Not nice hot milk. Why, I'd just as soon
Eat a silkworm wrapped in a white cocoon.

But seeing that she was my oldest kin,
I'd hoist high my sled and shuffle on in
With my shoes all wet and my socks aslosh
And I'd stomp globs of snowstorm off each galosh.

You know, it was funny: against my will,
That milk, hot and steamy, would drive back my chill
And out of that kitchen coal stove would steal
As glad a glow as a kid could feel,

And my grandma would hum an old-country song
That sounded as though put together wrong,
But it landed on me with a lifting lilt
As I sat wrapped round in a patchwork quilt.

Friends

BRAVES

My friend Mark, he's one special boy—
A real live fifth-grade Iroquois
And once I saw in all the papers
About his dad, who builds skyscrapers.

Some architects ran out of luck:
Atop a half-built building, stuck,
They stood there scared and hollered murder
Till Mark's dad coolly climbed a girder.

Against the sky, up where it's scary,
He walked as if he walked a prairie.
Unruffled as a bird's sleek wings,
He lowered them in firemen's slings.

When he grows up, Mark says he dreams,
He'll skywalk too and weld steel beams—
That's not a life I'd greet with raves.
Guess only Indians are braves.

WHO TO TRADE STAMPS WITH

Who to trade stamps with?
Don't hurry. Be a chooser.

The kind that finds Malawi on a map,
He's a nice kind.

The kind that likes just prices,
He's a loser.

TELEPHONE TALK

Back flat on the carpet,
Cushion under my head,
Sock feet on the wallpaper,
Munching raisin bread,

Making easy whispers
Balance on high wire,
Trading jokes and laughing,
The two of us conspire,

Closer than when walking
Down the street together,
Closer than two sparrows
Hiding from wet weather.

How would my shrill whistle
Sound to you, I wonder?
Give a blow in *your* phone,
My phone makes it thunder.

Through the night, invisibly
Jumping over space,
Back and forth between us
All our secrets race.

MY STUPID PARAKEET
NAMED AFTER YOU
(from a letter to a best friend)

You know my stupid parakeet
Named after you? (He has big feet.)
Well, he cracked his beak. Ran into a lamp.
The vet applied a little clamp.

But that's not all. Whenever he naps,
He falls right off his perch and flaps
So hard he almost flies apart.
Compared to that dumb bird, you're smart.

BIG SAUL FEIN

A man I'd call tremendous—that's
Our neighbor, tall Saul Fein.
Why, all the gadgets in his house
Are of his own design.

He studies everything there is;
His memory's like a giant's.
He's always listening to a book.
He helps me do my science.

He speaks in prisons, old folks' homes—
Dad says Saul has a heart
As large as he is. Being big
Is what sets him apart.

That's why, to help him cross the street
And be his seeing eyes,
It takes no *little* dog, but one
Who's extra-large in size.

LOULEEN'S FEELINGS

You know, I'm a little ashamed
To bring those white kids home
To our third-floor walk-up—
I mean, those cats like big-apartment trips.
Well, my house has a toilet always runs,
A faucet drips.

Of course, it's *clean,* and all, and clean comes hard
On account of Momma working every day
Except half-Saturdays. But white
Cats like big stereos and VCRs,
They like to get a ride home in cool cars—
I know one even has a swimming pool
That lights up green for swimming in at night.

Well, I just can't compete
Except, that is, in school.
I don't mind being president of my class.
And Momma, she keeps me into real fine clothes—
She says, "Oh, Lord, that's where my money goes."
They don't make any courses I can't pass.

Sure, if they came, I bet they'd act real kind
And look around and find lots to forgive.
But where it's at is who and what you are,
Not only what you have, not where you live.

THE GIRL WHO MAKES THE CYMBALS BANG

I'm the girl who makes the cymbals bang—
It used to be a boy
That got to play them in the past
Which always would annoy

Me quite a bit. Though I complained,
Our teacher Mister Cash
Said, "Sorry, girls don't have the strength
To come up with a crash."

"Oh yeah?" said I. "Please give them here!"
And there and then, I slammed
Together those brass plates so hard
His eardrums traffic-jammed.

He gulped and gaped, and I could tell
His old ideas were bending—
So now me and my cymbals give
Each song a real smash ending.

MRS. MORIZAWA'S MORNING

Mrs. Morizawa,
Frail as the ancient fan
She brought to America
From Japan,

Brushes white forelocks
And rises, slow
As the steam from her kettle
On her stove turned low.

She feeds her canary,
Bows once to her cat.
She intones her prayers
On a worn reed mat,

Turns on the TV
And feels a pang
At an image of Mount Fuji
Where petals hang.

Oh, when will it jingle,
The bell on her phone?
Her daughter is distant,
She's quite alone.

Mrs. Morizawa,
Heron-thin,
Fingers a mole
On her still-smooth chin,

Reads an old love letter
With a faded stamp
Whose return address
Says *Internment Camp,*

Drifts through her garden
Where anemones stun
With their opening fragrance
The fresh day's sun,

To the pond of lilies
Where the small frog's asleep—
She walks softly, softly,
Lest he wake and leap.

Mrs. Morizawa
In the sun's warm gold
To her chair sinks as carefully
As a fan might fold.

Not So
Ordinary Things

POPPING POPCORN

How suddenly each tiny seed
Into a puffball grows!

A *ping, ping, ping* within the pan
Accelerates, then slows—

I like to lift the lid and look,
But if I do, it snows.

MOTE

Dust mote in a sunbeam,
I blow on you—you soar,
Revolving on your poles, a moon
For spacefolk to explore.

What will you show them? Roads of gold
Where dragons and dragonflies race?
A princess dressed in spidery silk
With moonlight all over her face?

When, tired of circling in the sun,
You care to spend the night,
Drift down. Take my fingertip
For your landing site.

METEOR SHOWER

On the hillside at night,
    A shooting star
Raked my path like the light
    From a passing car,

Then it switched off its beam
    And the world winked dark,
And I wondered. Who'd dream
    Stars would stop to park?

NIGHT FOG

Down by the docks
    In the dark, the foghorn
That mournfully croaks
    Might be called a froghorn.

In its tower by the river
    The lighthouse light
Like a steady power mower
    Keeps mowing night.

PAPERCLIPS

A jumbled sight,
The sheets I write!
      High time for paperclips
To take a bite
And grip them tight
      Between bright bulldog lips.

TEN LITTLE LIKENESSES

1

The fly's buzz:
a radio tuned
where no station was.

2

Six
black
appleseeds
sleek
as beetles' backs

mark

where the eaten
apple's
left its tracks.

3

When the stoplight
drops
from red
to green
cars leap
like shot slung
from a slingshot.

4

Like a bird
with salt on its tail,
the branch
freighted with snow
stands still.

5

River races
round its bend
like a pack
of black
cats,
dogs after them,
turning a corner.

6

It doesn't seem
to want to flow downstream,
this full
moon like a yellow
beachball.

7

Open-billed
gulls
fighting
for fish heads
creak
like
rusted
gates.

8

From the phone wires
in quick
alarm
a flock
of crows
explodes.

9

At the sun's
far
target
earth
flings
spears:

white birches.

10

The river
flows down
to its delta
and sets sail
on the sea.

LINES FOR REMEMBERING ABOUT LIDS

The way hands move around a clock
Is how hands make a jar lid lock.

Hands must go backwards, if they are
To make a jar lid come ajar.

TO A SNOWFLAKE

You stand still in midair
As though you just can't quite
Make up your wisher where
You wish to spend tonight.

THE KITE THAT BRAVED OLD ORCHARD BEACH

The kite that braved Old Orchard Beach
  But fell and snapped its spine
Hangs in our attic out of reach,
  All tangled in its twine.

My father says, "Let's throw it out,"
  But I won't let him. No,
There has to be some quiet spot
  Where cracked-up heroes go.

Birds, Beasts & Fish

WALKING BIG BO

To walk Big Bo our Saint Bernard
Around the block is kind of hard.

A mountain mounted on four wheels
With you in tow is how he feels.

He downhills fast as anything
And pulls you, hanging to his string.

Once when he spied a tiger cat
Big Bo took off in no time flat.

I stayed behind him all the while—
I must have run a minute mile.

It isn't strolling. More like stalking.
Which one is taking which one walking?

OBNOXIOUS NELLY

Whenever I stretch
Out to read the paper,
Nelly gives a meow
And decides to drape her

Over Pogo or Garfield
Like a striped fur coat—
She certainly knows
How to get my goat.

Just as soon as she spies
Mrs. Neighbor sunning
Her new baby in his buggy,
She comes a-running

And while people peer in,
Going *ah* and *ooh*,
That conniving cat
Grabs attention, too—

With a grasshopper leap,
Obnoxious Nelly
Squats and smiles and purrs
On the kid's potbelly.

GOLDFISH

Goldfish flash past, keeping busy,
Circling, circling till they're dizzy
Round the racetrack of their bowl—

Me, I'll take a swimming hole.

CRICKET

The cheerful cricket, when he sings
    To celebrate fall weather,
Lifts high the scrapers on his wings
    And fiddles them together

And when some juicy ant he sees,
    His bulby eyeballs glisten.
He tucks his ears beneath his knees
    And lifts a leg to listen.

Imagine—what if you or I
    Were laid out like a cricket
And had an ear beside our knee?
    That might be just the ticket,

For if you didn't want to hear
    The loudest band that rocks,
Why, all you'd do to shut your ears
    Is yank up both your socks.

TO A TUNA

Hey, tuna fish, you know, I wish
You came with head and tail.
You turn out can-shaped on a dish
Like wet sand from a pail.

Which makes me wonder. Are you just
One big long log or eel?
I guess I'm fond of you, all right,
But can you be for real?

THE TABLES TURNED

Over the hill with a horrible growl, running
  lickety-split due south,
The galloping Doberman pinscher goes, with our
  tomcat Tom in his mouth,
Our poor old Tom that's done nobody harm, with
  his crookety tail so dapper,
Now only today he's been carried away by the
  neighborhood catnapper.

Oh, I won't chase after the two of them, for fear of
  what I'll find.
Let's call for an ambulance, firemen, police,
  anybody—why, never mind!
For here they come galloping home again, and—what
  a surprise for a clincher—
Our Tom small and frail has his teeth in the tail of
  that big bully Doberman pinscher!

A LESSON

He made fun of my Pekingese:
Call that a dog? What knobby knees!

I'd take her walking on a leash—
Hey look! There goes a furry quiche!
I bet she polishes her nails!
Where did she come from? Bloomingdale's?

Well, my Pekingese beat up his mutt
And now he keeps his big mouth shut.

COTTON-BOTTOMED MENACE

That rabbit in my garden patch
Knows how to chew, chomp, snip, and snatch,
Yank sleeping carrots from their beds
And leave my spring-long work in shreds.

I don't much mind it if we share
Some lettuce leaves—I've loads to spare.
He's welcome to a little bite,
But *that* guy—he's pure appetite!

DODOS

I'd like to know what hit the dodo bird.
It sang a song that, lately, no one's heard.

We don't know why. I'd guess, for what it's worth,
That something dodos did so irked the earth

It told those birds to buzz off into space
And leave the planet to a smarter race.

Well, here we are. But now that acid rain's
Souring lakes, I think, What's with our brains?

And when I read that porpoises and whales
Have trappers and harpooners on their trails,

That of all earth's polluters we're the chief,
I say we'd best turn over a new leaf

Or else another race, some later comer,
Will write that we were dodos, only dumber.

Times of Year

NEW YEAR'S ADVICE FROM MY CORNISH GRANDMOTHER

In Cornwall, England, on New Year's Eve, people thought riches would come their way if they placed silver on their doorsteps overnight. They also thought it bad luck to let in a visitor with red hair on New Year's morning.

On New Year's Eve, at your front door
Set out a silver pin
To fetch inside on New Year's morn
That riches may come in.

And in the new year, oh, don't dare
(Lest all your year be curst)
Let any person with red hair
Step past your doorsill first!

Let who is eldest first break fast
And let the baby sleep,
Then dust away the old year's dust
And kiss a chimney sweep.

MARTIN LUTHER KING DAY

Solemn bells in steeples sing:

Doctor
Martin
Luther
King.

He lived his life
He dreamed his dream:
The worst-off people
To redeem,

He dreamed a world
Where people stood
Not separate, but
In brotherhood.

Now ten-ton bells together swing:

Remember
Martin
Luther
King.

SONG FOR A VALENTINE

Just the way a boat needs a wave to toss it,
Just the way a moat needs a drawbridge to cross it,
Just the way a goat needs a drinking-water faucet—
That's the way I need you.

Just the way a fisherman needs a net to haul on,
Just the way a crab needs a beach to crawl on,
Just the way a tree needs a lumberjack to fall on—
That's the way I need you.

Just the way a spoon needs a cup of coffee,
Just the way cough syrup needs a throat that's
  coughy,
Just the way a jaw needs a glob of chewy toffee—
That's the way I need you.

Just the way a car needs a left-turn blinker,
Just the way a fish needs hook, line, and sinker,
Just the way a park needs a statue of *The Thinker*—
That's the way I need you.

Just the way a baseball needs a mitt to catch it,
Just the way an itch needs a hand to scratch it,
Just the way a door needs a latch to latch it,
That's the way I need you.

Just the way a bike needs a pusher on its pedal,
Just the way a loom needs a tromper on its treadle,

Just the way a runner needs a bright bronze medal—
That's the way I need you.

Just the way a mouse needs a nibble of cheddar,
Just the way a house needs a grass-seed spreader,
Just the way a steep snowy slope needs a sledder—
That's the way I need you.

Just the way a finger needs a sewing thimble,
Just the way a drummer needs a loud crash-cymbal,
Just the way a candlestick needs Jack-be-nimble—
That's the way I need you.

Just the way F-sharp needs a horn to blow it,
Just the way a cabbage needs a hoe to hoe it,
Just the way a blank hunk of paper needs a poet—
That's the way I need you.

Just the way a bulldog needs a leg to bite on,
Just the way a flea needs a dog to light on,
Just the way a ship needs a star to sight on—
That's the way I need you.

MARCH THAW

When lakes grow too limber
    For skates, when sled bites
Bare dirt, causing tumbles,
    When ice stalactites

Plunge streetward to splinter,
    When rooftops let slip
Whole snow-mountains, winter
    Is losing its grip.

When snowmen, long frozen,
    From wet noses weep,
A whole slippery season
    Starts sliding to sleep.

AFTER EASTER SNOW

Whoever egged our house on Halloween
    (We heard them cackle, making their escapes)
Lay down in snow, wagged arms, and rose again,
    Printing our lawn with wide-winged angel shapes.

CHOCOLATE RABBIT

An eight-inch rabbit—just my size!
He blinks pink-pupiled sugar eyes
And grins a bright white grin of cheer
As if to say, "Break off my ear,
Please do." What hard-heart could resist?
All right, I will. If you insist.

One lonesome ear—that looks a mite
Lopsided. Perhaps I'd better bite
The other off to even things—
Crunch. But this disappearance brings
A problem: someone should have stitched
That gaping gap where ears once twitched,
But since I'm feeling underfed
I'll help him out—off with his head!

He seems, now, just a one-inch rabbit.
Like him, I've got the nibbling habit.
There's not much left of him to savor—
Poor Bun. I'll do him one last favor.

SUMMER COOLER

In the summer young Angus McQuade
Carries off to his castle of shade
    Two cool soothing pillows,
    The Wind in the Willows,
And an ocean of iced lemonade.

WISHING FOR WINTER IN SUMMER

Why won't it snow in summer?
I wish there was a wizard
Who'd wave his wand and say the word
And sock us with a blizzard.

I've swum so much I'm half dissolved.
I'm tired of riding bicycles.
I want to throw a snowball and
Knock down some rooftop icicles.

You can't make snowmen out of grass—
That just won't get you far.
I want to see my dad put chains
And snow tires on the car.

I want to hear the firehouse horn
Go *Bawp! No school today*,
Roll over, and go back to sleep
And dream of summer play.

JACK-O'-LANTERN

The stick of a stem
    In his hat for a handle,
He grins a gold gleam
    From a flickering candle.

What a kitchen-knife leer
    Someone's carved in his jaw!
Jagged teeth like the teeth
    Of a carpenter's saw,

Sharp triangular eyes
    That can cast a spell—
I'll bet nobody knows
    He's a hollow shell.

AT PLYMOUTH

The First Thanksgiving, 1621

From friendly Squanto, wise in all things wild,
We found out where the fattest codfish flash.
To mingle beans and corn in succotash—
He schooled us well, as though we were his child.

Today we lay our feast on maple planks
Before Chief Massasoyt and ninety braves.
Now out of barrels bound by stout oak staves
We draw a drink to raise in heartfelt thanks

For turkey-cock, ripe pumpkin, squash, and gourd,
For stalks that stand all ears in heavy row,
For fallow deer that round the woodlands go—
Praise to thee, Lord!

By winter winds whose edges carve like knives
Our numbers have been pared.
Now we who have been spared
Thank the good Lord who took but half our lives.

SETTING THE THANKSGIVING TABLE

Fetch bouquets of bittersweet.
Give them to wild birds to eat.

Bring the homely freckled gourd.
Let it ornament our board.

Bring the pumpkin plump in shape,
Bring the perfect purple grape,

Pile the polished apples high,
Granny Smith and Northern Spy,

Bring the chestnut in its fur
Coat of bristly brownish burr,

Bring in sun-bleached stalks, each ear
Ripe and golden as the year.

Bring, each day you wake and live,
Fresh supplies of thanks to give.

EARTH'S BIRTHDAY

Come to the earth's
Birthday party,
Artie, in your Woolworth's
Party hat. Limber
Your voice up, Joyce,
All set to sing.

Will they stick oak trees
In for candles,
Wrap a breeze
In tissue paper, send
For a few new animals?
Blow up a cloud and tie
It with a string?

When is the earth's
Birthday? Well, today.
But so
Is every day!